FU~~NNY~~
JOKES
and
FOXY
RIDDLES

illustrated by ALLAN JAFFEE

KATHY SEIDEL

 GOLDEN PRESS • NEW YORK

FUNNY JOKES AND FOXY RIDDLES

CUSTOMER: When I bought this cat, you told me he was good for mice. He doesn't go near them.

CLERK: Well, isn't that good for mice?

DOCTOR: Did you go to another doctor before you came to me?

PATIENT: No, I went to a druggist.

DOCTOR: What foolish advice did he give you?

PATIENT: He told me to come to you.

OLD LADY: A ticket to Toledo, please.

TICKET AGENT: Do you want to go by Buffalo?

OLD LADY: No, better make it by train.

MARY WROTE TO TOM: If you don't get this letter, let me know and I'll write another one.

WAITRESS: What would you like for dinner, sir?
CUSTOMER: A hot dog.
WAITRESS: With pleasure!
CUSTOMER: No, with mustard!

HUSBAND: Honey, this lettuce tastes funny.
WIFE: It shouldn't. It's clean. I even washed it with soap.

MILKMAN: Are you sure you want 54 quarts of milk?
LADY: Yes, my doctor told me to take a bath in milk.
MILKMAN: Do you want it pasteurized?
LADY: No, just up to my chin.

CITY SLICKER: I saved my money and bought a farm ten miles long and half an inch wide.
FARMER: What are you going to raise on it?
CITY SLICKER: Spaghetti.

How many letters are there in the alphabet?

Eleven—t-h-e a-l-p-h-a-b-e-t.

What is round and purple, travels in
a long, black limousine, and car-
ries a machine gun?

Al Caplum.

There are seven maple trees and on
the seven maple trees are seven
branches and on the seven branches
are seven acorns. How many acorns
are there?

None. Acorns don't grow on maple
trees.

What starts with "T," is full of "T"
and ends with "T"?

A teapot.

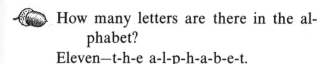

What's red and goes "puff, puff"?
An outboard apple!

What's a volcano?
A mountain with hiccups.

What's green and pecks on trees?
Woody Woodpickle.

 Why is the figure 9 like a peacock?
Because without its tail it is nothing.

 What is a bull when he is sleeping?
A bull dozer.

 What did one candle say to the other?
Are you going out tonight?

What's green and goes slam, slam, slam, slam?
A four-door pickle.

DAN: Dad, is it true that the law of gravity keeps us on our planet?
DAD: Yes.
DAN: What did we do before the law was passed?

WIT: I haven't slept for ten days.
NIT: Aren't you tired?
WIT: No, I sleep nights.

TEACHER: Use the word "geometry" in a sentence.
BOB: The little acorn grew and grew, and one day it awoke and said, "Gee-ahm-a-tree."

TEACHER: What is a comet?
LULU: A star with a tail.
TEACHER: Name one.
LULU: Lassie!

LIBRARIAN: Please be quiet. The people next to you can't read.
LITTLE BOY: What a shame! I've been reading since I was six.

NIT: It's raining cats and dogs.
WIT: I know. I just stepped in a poodle!

A farmer and his wife went to a fair. The farmer was fascinated by the airplanes and finally asked a pilot how much a ride cost.

"Ten dollars for three minutes," the pilot said. "But I'll make you a deal. If you and your wife can ride without making a sound, it will cost nothing, but if you say one word, you have to pay ten dollars."

"Agreed," said the farmer.

They went for the ride and after the pilot landed, he said, "I want to congratulate you for not making a sound. You are a very brave man."

"Maybe so," said the farmer, "but I almost yelled when my wife fell out."

REGGIE: What are you taking for your cold?
DICK: I don't know. How much will you give me?

A banana truck weighed one ton; the bananas weighed 350 pounds; the first man on the truck weighed 120 pounds. What did the second man weigh?
He weighed the bananas!

What has two feet on each side and one in the middle?
A yardstick!

What is green and sings?
Elvis Parsley.

How do you catch a rabbit?
You stand behind a bush and make a noise like a carrot.

When should a baker stop making doughnuts?

When he gets tired of the hole business.

Why did the crow sit on the telephone line?

Because he was making a long distance caw.

What is the best way to make a coat last?

Make the pants first.

Name an outstanding feat of the Romans.

Speaking Latin!

What did the robot say to the gas pump?

Take your finger out of your ear and listen to me.

What's green and very dangerous?
A frog with a hand-grenade.

What happens to ducks that fly upside down?
They quack up.

GIRL AT COUNTER: I'd like a triple chocolate ice cream sundae with lots of nuts and whipped cream.
SODA JERK: With a cherry on top?
GIRL: Golly, no! I'm on a diet!

NIT: Do you know how deep that river is?
WIT: It must be shallow because it only goes up to that duck's stomach.

A lawyer was in a dentist chair ready to get his tooth pulled and he said, "Do you swear to pull the tooth and nothing but the tooth?"

Does your clock tell time?
No. You have to look at it.

LADY IN A PET SHOP: How much is that canary?
CLERK: Five dollars.
LADY: Good. Send me the bill.
CLERK: Can't do that, lady. You have to take the whole bird!

TEACHER: Give me a sentence using the word "politics."
STUDENT: A parrot named Polly swallowed a watch, and now Polly ticks.

FIRST CANNIBAL: I don't care for your friend.
SECOND CANNIBAL: O.K., just eat the vegetables!

STEVE: I've been seeing spots before my eyes.

BRUCE: Did you see a doctor?

STEVE: No, just spots.

What is white outside, green inside, and hops?

A frog sandwich.

What goes ninety-nine, thump, ninety-nine, thump?

A centipede with a wooden leg.

What is gray, has four legs, a tail and a trunk?

A mouse going on a trip.

What were Tarzan's last words?

Who greased the grape vine!

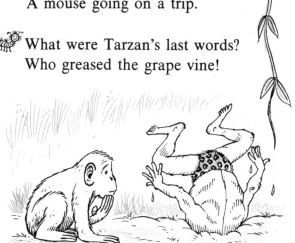

Why did Santa Claus use only seven reindeer this year?
He left Comet home to clean the sink.

What kind of monkeys grow on stems?
Gray apes.

What's six feet long, green, and has eight eyes?
The Jolly Green Giant's sneakers!

What are baby monster's parents called?
Dead and Mummy.

How do you make soup gold?
You put in 14 carrots.

What's a raisin?
A worried grape.

What's a Grecian urn?
It depends on what kind of work he does.

Hickory, dickory, dock,
Three mice ran up the clock.
The clock struck one . . .
And the other two escaped with minor injuries!

DISPENSARY

The absent-minded professor thought he had left his watch at home, so he pulled it out of his pocket to see if he had time to go home before class to get it.

NIT: A snake snapped at me.
WIT: Snakes don't snap. They strike.
NIT: This one was a garter snake.

TEACHER: How did this window get broken?
LITTLE BOY: I was cleaning my slingshot and it went off.

TEACHER: What happened in 1809?
JOHN: Lincoln was born.
TEACHER: Now, what happened in 1812?
JOHN: He had his third birthday!

An Indian chief and his son stood on a high mountain. The chief held his hand over the great prairie and said, "Son, someday Indians own all this land again. White man all go to moon."

Did you hear about the cross-eyed teacher?
Yes, she had trouble with her pupils.

ROB: How's your girl friend coming with her diet?
BOB: She's disappeared!

PROFESSOR, RAPPING ON DESK: Order, please!
SLEEPY VOICE FROM BACK ROW: Hamburger with onions for me.

When does ten plus ten equal ten?
When you add it wrong.

What animal has the smallest appetite?
A moth. It just eats holes.

When is a clock at the head of the
stairs dangerous?
When it runs down and strikes one!

What did Paul Revere say at the end
of his ride?
Whoa!

Tell me two things you can never eat
for breakfast.
Lunch and dinner!

Why did the rocket lose its job?
It got fired!

19

What would you do if you ran out of gas in the jungle?

Put a tiger in your tank.

A man lived on one side of the river, and the store was on the other side. The bridge across the river could hold only 200 pounds. The man weighed 198 pounds, and he bought 3 coconuts that weighed 1 pound each. How did he get across the bridge?

The man juggled the coconuts. One was always in the air.

How did the firefly feel when he ran into a fan?

He was delighted!

Why does Santa Claus have a garden?

Because he likes to Ho, Ho, Ho!

What is the most disagreeable month to a soldier?

A long March!

MAN IN A HURRY: Will the hotcakes be long?
WAITER: No, round, as usual!

LITTLE BOY: I'd like to buy that dog, but his legs are too short.
CLERK: Too short? Why, all four of them touch the ground!

NIT: Did you take a bath today?
WIT: Why, is one missing?

PETE: My mother knit my brother in the army three socks.
TONY: Why *three* socks?
PETE: My brother wrote and said he had grown another foot.

21

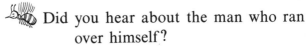 Did you hear about the man who ran over himself?

No, how did it happen?

No one would go to the store for him so he ran over himself.

TEACHER: There will be an eclipse of the moon tonight. Perhaps your parents will let you stay up and watch it.

PUPIL: What channel?

ANN: I spent 10 hours over my math book last night.

BILL: You did?

ANN: Yes, it fell under my bed.

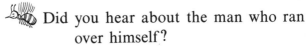 What will soon be the largest city in the world?

Dublin, Ireland, because it is always doublin'.

NIT: What do you like to put in a sandwich?

WIT: My teeth!

What goes "zzub, zzub"?
A bee flying backwards!

What does a chicken do when it stands on one leg?
Lifts the other leg up!

What did the porcupine say to the cactus?
Is that you, Mama?

What's a boobee bug?
It's a bug that sneaks up behind a bee and says, "Boo, Bee!"

What did the eye say to the ice cube?
Icy you!

What is hard to beat?
A drum with a hole in it.

23

What did the boy octopus say to the girl octopus?

I want to hold your hand, hand, hand, hand, hand, hand, hand, hand.

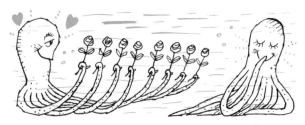

HUNTER: I spotted a leopard.

HIS WIFE: Don't be silly, dear. They grow that way.

What did the ram say to his sweetheart?

I love ewe.

Why did 28 men suddenly walk out of the restaurant?

They had finished eating.

RESTAURANT

When was beef the highest?
When the cow jumped over the moon.

BOY (WITH SHAGGY HAIR): Are you the barber who cut my hair the last time?
BARBER: Couldn't be. I've only been here for three months!

WIT: What's the difference between an elephant and a matterbaby?
NIT: What's a matterbaby?
WIT: Nothing. What's the matter with you?

FARMER: How did you come to fall in the pond?
TOMMY: I didn't come to fall in. I came to fish.

TEACHER: If I take five apples from ten apples, what's the difference?
STUDENT: That's what I say—what's the difference?

NIT: I hear that Margie and Harry had some hot words. Is it true?

WIT: Yes, she threw a bowl of alphabet soup at him.

JACK: Did I ever tell you about the time I came face to face with a lion?

JOAN: No, what happened?

JACK: There I stood, without a gun. The lion growled and crept closer . . . closer . . . closer . . .

JOAN: Gosh, what did you do?

JACK: I moved on to the next cage!

BABY CORN: Mommy, who brought me?

MOTHER CORN: The stalk brought you!

BOB: "Sugar" is the only word in English where the *su* sounds like *sh*.

BETTY: Are you *sure?*

Why is the sea measured in knots?
To keep the ocean tide.

If you put a mother duck and five ducklings in a box, what would you have?
A box of quackers.

What's the hardest thing about learning to roller skate?
The pavement.

Why is the grass dangerous?
It is full of blades.

What's so fabulous about a tiny TV set?
Tiny commercials.

Why do men wear watches when they go to the desert?
Because each one has a spring in it.

What is the best way to keep a skunk from smelling?
Hold his nose.

What is a bee?
Just a little humbug.

What is pigskin used for most?
To hold pigs together.

What goes "Oom! Oom!"?
A cow walking backwards.

Why did the hen cross the street?
To see a man lay bricks.

DENTIST: What kind of filling do you want in your tooth?

MARY: Chocolate.

STUDENT: I don't think I deserve a zero on my paper!

TEACHER: I don't either, but it's the lowest mark I have!

TEACHER: Bob, did your father write this story?

BOB: No. He started it, but Mom had to do it over!

NIT: Were the test questions hard?

WIT: Oh, the questions were easy. It was the answers that I had trouble with.

Two moving van men were taking things into a house. One said, "Joe, help me lift this chest."

Joe asked, "Why? Did Miss Jones tell you to?"

"No," replied Tom.

"Then how do you know she wants it moved?" asked Joe.

"Because she's under it."

BROTHER: What are you doing, Sis?
SISTER: Writing a letter to my cousin.
BROTHER: Why are you writing so slowly?
SISTER: He can't read very fast.

CUSTOMER: What is this fly doing in my soup?
WAITER: The back stroke!

SUE: Mom, may I have ten cents for a man who is crying outside?
MOM: What is he crying about?
SUE: Ice cream only ten cents.

NIT: Must you make so much noise?
WIT: How can I play tennis without a racket?

"Knock, knock!"
"Who's there?"
"Banana."
"Banana who?"
"Knock, knock!"
"Who's there?"
"Banana."
"Banana who?"
"Knock, knock!"
"Who's there?"
"Banana."
"Banana who?"
"Knock, knock!"
"Who's there?"
"Orange."
"Orange who?"
"Orange you glad I didn't say 'banana' again?"

"Knock, knock!"
"Who's there?"
"Hamen."
"Hamen who?"
"Hamen eggs."

"Knock, knock!"
"Who's there?"
"Cantaloupe."
"Cantaloupe who?"
"Cantaloupe tonight. Dad has the car!"

"Knock, knock!"
"Who's there?"
"Amos."
"Amos who?"
"A mosquito bit me."
"Knock, knock!"
"Who's there?"
"Andy."
"Andy who?"
"And he bit me again!"

BOB: My father made such a good scarecrow that the crows won't come near our farm.

ANN: My dad beat that. His scarecrow is so good that the crows brought back all the corn they stole last year!

 "I have a baseball dog."
"What makes you say that?"
"He catches flies and fowls and runs for home when the catcher comes."

CHILD MONSTER: Mom, I just knocked over the ladder in the garden.

MOTHER MONSTER: You'd better tell your father.

CHILD MONSTER: He knows. He was on the ladder at the time.

PATTY: Did you know that it takes three sheep to make one sweater?

MATTY: No, I didn't even know they could knit.

33

"Hello, is this the office of Livingston, Livingston, Livingston, and Livingston, Attorneys at Law?"

"Yes, it is."

"May I please speak to Mr. Livingston?"

"Sorry, he's in court."

"May I please speak to Mr. Livingston?"

"Sorry, he's in conference."

"May I please speak to Mr. Livingston?"

"Sorry, he's on vacation."

"May I please speak to Mr. Livingston?"

"Speaking!"

BOY: Dad, are you growing taller?

DAD: No, why?

BOY: Because your head is sticking through your hair!

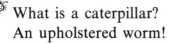 What is a caterpillar?
An upholstered worm!

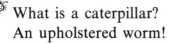 What do you call a rabbit with a lot
of fleas?
Bugs Bunny!

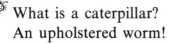 What did the necktie say to the hat?
You go on a head and I'll hang around.

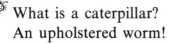 Which is bigger—Mr. Bigger or Mr. Bigger's baby?
The baby, of course, because he's a little Bigger.

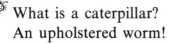 What's the difference between a teacher and a train?
A teacher says, "Spit out your gum!"
A train says, "Choo, choo!"

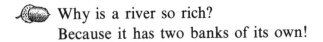 Why is a river so rich?
Because it has two banks of its own!

What did the nearsighted porcupine say when it backed into a cactus?
Pardon me, honey.

Why did the little boy put hay in his bed?
To feed his nightmare.

Why is a person's nose always in the middle of his face?
Because it is the scenter.

Why isn't your nose 12 inches long?
Because then it would be a foot.

When does a man have four hands?
When he doubles his fists.

MOTHER: How did you do on your first day of school?

TOMMY: Not so well, I guess. I have to go back tomorrow.

MOTHER: Everything is going up . . . the price of food, toys, everything. I wish something would go down!

DAUGHTER: Take a look at my report card!

COWBOY: Did you find the horse well behaved?

CITY TENDERFOOT: I should say so! Whenever we came to a fence, he let me over first!

SNOB: My ancestors came over on the Mayflower.

SLOB: It's lucky for them. Immigration laws are stricter now.

A GUEST IN THE HOUSE SAID: You're cleaning up the spilled coffee with cake!

MAN: It's sponge cake.

TEACHER: Sally, tell me where the elephant is found.

SALLY: Teacher, the elephant is such a large animal that it is scarcely ever lost.

OLD MAN: How old are you, sonny?

SMALL BOY: Six.

OLD MAN: Six! Why you're not as tall as my cane.

SMALL BOY: How old is your cane?

NIT: How do you keep a dog off the road?

WIT: Put him in a Barking Lot.

A motorist, following a tail light in a dense fog, crashed into the car ahead of him when it stopped suddenly. "Why didn't you let me know when you were going to stop?" he yelled. "Why should I?" said a voice. "I'm in my own garage."

Why did the boy ghost whistle at the
girl ghost?
Because she was boo-tiful!

What did one ghost say to the other?
Do you believe in people?

What do ghosts eat for dinner?
Spook-getti.

SHLOORP

What did the mother ghost say to the
baby ghost?
Don't spook until spooken to.

What do spooks call their navy?
The Ghost Guard.

What do ghosts eat for breakfast?
Ghost Toasties.

What does a ghost on guard duty say
when he hears a noise?
Halt! Who ghost there?

What do ghosts chew?
Boo-ble gum.

TEACHER: Name a collective noun.
PUPIL: Garbage truck.

"I beg your pardon," the man said to
the Indian, "what's your name?"
"Running Deer," said the Indian.
"Is that your son?"
"Yes."
"What's his name?"
"Ninety-eight cents."
"Ninety-eight cents?"
"Yes, he's not a buck yet."

VIC: When my dad was in Africa he caught a Lion twenty feet long.
VERA: Some lyin'!

COFFEE—something your parents need in the morning before you make any noise.
OCEAN—where buoy meets gull.
T.V.—a watching machine.

DAD: Bill, wash your face! I can see what you had for breakfast this morning.
BILL: What did I have?
DAD: Eggs.
BILL: Wrong. That was yesterday.

CITY LADY: Look at that bunch of cows.
COWBOY: No, herd.
CITY LADY: Heard of what?
COWBOY: Herd of cows.
CITY LADY: Sure, I've heard of cows!
COWBOY: No, a cow herd.
CITY LADY: What do I care what a cow heard? I've got no secrets from a cow!

41

Why did the moron bring a ladder to a football game?
He wanted to see the Giants play.

Why can't you drive a golf ball?
It doesn't have a steering wheel.

What day of the year is a command to go forward?
March 4th!

What is worse than a giraffe with a sore throat?
A centipede with corns.

Why can't a bicycle stand by itself?
Because it's two-tired.

Why are the medieval centuries called the Dark Ages?
Because it was Knight time.

What is blue, flies, and is dangerous?
A bluebird with a gun!

When are cooks cruel?
When they beat the eggs and whip the cream!

What did one tonsil say to the other?
Get dressed; the doctor's taking us out tonight!

What did the Indian say when his dog fell over the cliff?
Dog-gone!

TAX COLLECTOR: Why don't you pay your taxes with a smile?

TAXPAYER: I'd love to but you insist on money.

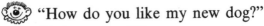 "How do you like my new dog?"
"Is he trained?"
"Of course! When I tell him not to sit up—he doesn't sit up!"

Have you heard about the new doctor doll?
You wind it up and it operates on batteries.

MAN: What's the matter, Miss?
GIRL: I lost my glasses and I can't look for them until I find them.

WIT: Did you ever tickle a mule?
NIT: No, why?
WIT: You should try it. You'll get a big kick out of it.

BOB: Did you change the water in the goldfish bowl?
ROB: They didn't drink it all yet.

"Can you lend me $500?"
"I only have $400."
"That's all right, you can owe me the other hundred!"

TEACHER: Carol, use "beetles" in a sentence.
CAROL: "By George," said John, "I think Paul's lost his Ringo."

TEACHER: Mindy, do you know what "climate" means?
MINDY: That's what most boys do when they see a ladder.

DOCTOR: What seems to be your trouble?
JONES: I have trouble breathing.
DOCTOR: Here's something to stop that.

What did Batman wear when he went swimming?
A batting suit.

Where did Batman plant his flowers?
In a batanical garden.

Why does Batman brush his teeth with Gleem?
To help prevent bat breath.

Why does Batman walk around in his pajamas?
He doesn't have a batrobe.

What did they say about Batman when he went crazy?
He has bells in his batfry.

What did they call Batman when he worked in the state department?

A diplobat.

FIRST SALESMAN: My job is selling salt.
SECOND SALESMAN: Why, that's my job, too!
FIRST SALESMAN: Shake.

A cowboy riding his horse saw a little dog running down the road.

"Hi," said the dog.

"Hi," said the cowboy.

A few moments later the cowboy said out loud, "That's funny. I didn't know dogs could talk!"

The horse turned his head, looked at the cowboy, and said, "You learn something new every day."

PRIZE FIGHTER'S SON: My pop is stronger than yours!
TRAFFIC COP'S SON: Oh, yeah? My pop can hold back a line of cars with one hand!

JIM: Teacher, would you spank me for something I didn't do?

TEACHER: Why no, Jim, why?

JIM: Well, I didn't do my math.

JIM: Your pants look very sad today.

BOB: What do you mean?

JIM: De-pressed!

MR. B.: Doctor, will I be able to read with these glasses?

DOCTOR: Yes.

MR. B.: Good! I've never been able to read before.

Why is a woman on a deserted island like a woman in a store?
She is always looking for a sail.

What would the nation be if all the cars were red?
A red car nation!

What is the best paper to make a kite out of?
Fly paper!

What did one eye say to the other eye?
Between us there's something that smells!

What's the difference between a fish and a piano?
You can't tuna fish!

What's black and white and red all over?
A bashful zebra!

What did one knight say to the other?
I don't mind jousting with you, Lancelot, but why do you keep yelling, "Stronger than dirt"?

Why was the mother flea crying?
Because her children had gone to the dogs.

What is the best way to catch a fish?
Have someone throw it to you.

What would you call a man who is always wiring for money?
An electrician!

What do bees do with their honey?
They cell it.

MOTHER LION: Junior, what are you doing?
BABY LION: I'm chasing a hunter around a tree.
MOTHER LION: How many times have I told you not to play with your food!

"My brother fell off a seven-foot tree."
"Did he get hurt?"
"No, he'd only climbed up one foot!"

NEW NEIGHBOR: Have you lived here all your life?
OLD TIMER: Not yet.

PILOT: Do you wanna fly?
BOY: You bet!
PILOT: Wait a minute, I'll catch one for you.

WAITER: How did you find your steak?
CUSTOMER: I looked under a mushroom and
there it was!

SIGN IN FRONT OF A HOME: Anyone's wel-
come to use our lawnmower, provided
he doesn't take it out of our yard.

PRISONER: Look! I'm free! I'm free!
LITTLE BOY: So what! I'm four!

JEAN: Why does your dog turn around so
many times before he lies down?
JANE: He's a watch dog, and he's winding
himself up.

MAMA OWL: I'm worried about Junior.
PAPA OWL: What's the matter?
MAMA OWL: Well, he just doesn't give a
hoot about anything.

An airplane and a helicopter were going
  fishing.

AIRPLANE: I'll get the fishing poles. You get
  the bait.

HELICOPTER: Why do I have to get the bait?

AIRPLANE: Everybody knows the whirlybird
  gets the worm.

Why did the teenage girl want her
  father to quit his job?
He was a beetle exterminator.

FATHER: When I see you in that Beatle
  jacket, I have to laugh.

DAUGHTER: Good, I'll put it on when you
  get the bill.

Why do people use Beatle soap?
To wash away the ringos.

What did the Beatles say when they saw an avalanche?

Here come The Rolling Stones.

What did Ringo say when he fell off the cliff?

I Want to Hold Your Hand.

JERRY: That's only a little green snake.
MARY: Yes, but it may be just as dangerous as a ripe one.

MOTHER PIGEON (TO SON): Watch your posture—you're beginning to walk people-toed!

SUSIE: Is that a real diamond ring?
MARGE: If it isn't, I've been cheated out of 29¢

WIT: With which hand do you stir your coffee?
NIT: My right, of course.
WIT: I use a spoon.

MAN: Did you hear who's in the hospital?
LADY: No. Who?
MAN: Mr. Ajax with ammonia.

JIM: I can prove that you aren't here.
LEON: How?
JIM: You aren't in New York, right? You aren't in Chicago, right? You aren't in Florida, right? If you aren't in those three places, you must be some place else, right? If you're some place else, then it's impossible to be here.

A teen-age boy who was falling in love went to the library and took out a book entitled "How to Hug." When he got home he found that he had volume 10 of the encyclopedia.

WOMAN: (opening the door of her refrigerator and finding a rabbit inside) What are you doing there?
RABBIT: This is a Westinghouse, isn't it?
WOMAN: Yes.
RABBIT: Well, I'm just "westing."

PSYCHIATRIST: Why do you always snap your fingers?
LITTLE BOY: To keep the tigers away.
PSYCHIATRIST: There isn't a tiger in fifty miles of here.
LITTLE BOY: It sure works, doesn't it?

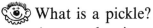 What is a pickle?
A cucumber in a sour mood.

A man got on his donkey and left to go to the mountains for a week. He left on Wednesday and returned on the same Wednesday. How did he do it?

His donkey was named Wednesday.

What has two ears, four feet, and tells time?

A watch dog.

Why didn't our government keep a record of the War of 1812?

Because the phonograph had not been invented yet.

What goes, "Ha, ha, ha, plop!"

Someone laughing his head off.

Why did the little moron go outdoors
with her purse open?
Because she was expecting some change
in the weather.

Why did Mickey Mouse take a trip to
outer space?
To find Pluto.

Why did the jelly roll?
It saw the apple turnover.

Why did Moses cross the Red Sea?
To avoid traffic.

What did the hen say when she saw a
plate of scrambled eggs?
What a bunch of mixed-up kids.

Why did the weatherman lose his job?
Because the weather didn't agree with
him.

BETTY: I wish I had enough money to buy an elephant.

BILLY: Why on earth do you want an elephant?

BETTY: I don't. I just want the money.

WHITE ELEPHANT SALE

Once there was an Indian chief named "Shortcake." The day he died, *squaw bury Shortcake.*

JEAN: What is the name of your dog?

MARY: Ginger.

JEAN: Does Ginger bite?

MARY: No, Ginger snaps.

DAD: Jack, what did you learn in school today?

JACK: I learned to say, "Yes, sir," "No, sir," "Yes, Ma'am," and "No, ma'am."

DAD: You did?

JACK: Yep!

JOHNNY: I fell over twenty feet last night.

GRANDMA: Mercy! Weren't you hurt?

JOHNNY: No, I was just trying to get to my seat in the movies.

MOTORIST: I've killed your cat, but I've come to replace him.

OLD LADY: Well, thank you very much, but do you think you can catch mice?

LADY: Please tell me which platform to go to for the train to Boston.

CONDUCTOR: Turn to the left and you'll be right.

LADY: Young man, don't be impertinent!

CONDUCTOR: Okay, then turn to the right and you'll be left!

BOB: Do you have time for a couple of dillys?

ROB: Sure, why not?

BOB: O.K. DILLY. DILLY.

"Knock, knock!"
"Who's there?"
"Tick."
"Tick who?"
"Tick um up, I'm a tongue-tied wobber."

"Knock, knock!"
"Who's there?"
"Sue."
"Sue who?"
"Sue Prize."

"Knock, knock!"
"Who's there?"
"Duane."
"Duane who?"
"Duane the bathtub. I'm dwowning!"

"Knock, knock!"
"Who's there?"
"Gladys."
"Gladys who?"
"Gladys Friday, how 'bout you?"

"Knock, knock!"
"Who's there?"
"Your Avon lady and your door bell
　　is broken."

"Knock, knock!"
"Who's there?"
"Tarzan."
"Tarzan who?"
"Tarzan Tripes Forever."

Pat and Bill were pushing a heavy hand-cart up a hill. Bill worked hard, but Pat did more leaning than pushing. Presently they stopped for a rest and Pat said, "Some push," as he looked down the hill. "Yes," replied Bill, "and some don't!"

NIT: What would you do if a man-eating tiger were chasing you?
WIT: Nothing. I'm a girl.

TEACHER (IN CHEMISTRY CLASS): What is the formula for water?
PUPIL: H-i-j-k-l-m-n-o.
TEACHER: Whoever told you that?
PUPIL: You did. You said it was H to O.

MAN (TO PSYCHIATRIST): Something's wrong with me. I keep thinking I'm a dog.

PSYCHIATRIST: How long has this been going on?

MAN: Since I was a puppy.

JOHNNY: More cake, please!

MOTHER: If you eat any more cake you'll burst.

JOHNNY: Pass the cake and get out of the way!

TEACHER: Children, there will be only a half day of school this morning.

PUPILS: Whoopee! Hooray!

TEACHER: Silence. We will have the other half this afternoon.

FATHER (PROUDLY): Don't you think our son gets his intelligence from me?

MOTHER: Probably. I know I still have mine.

HUSBAND: This coffee tastes like mud.

WIFE: Well, it was ground this morning.

What did the man say when he poured coke in his gas tank?
Things go better with coke.

What do you get when you cross a mink with a kangaroo?
A mink coat with pockets.

What did the little moron say when he saw some milk bottles in the grass?
Hey! I found a cow's nest.

What letter is not in the alphabet?
A letter in a mail box.

How do you catch a squirrel?
You climb a tree and act like a nut!

Where does a sheep get his hair cut?
At the baa-baa shop!

What is purple and lights up?
An electric grape.

What did the baby sardine say when he saw a submarine?
Look! There's a can of people!

Where is the monsters' favorite tourist spot?
The Vampire State Building.

How does a witch tell time?
With a witch watch.

If an Indian woman is a squaw, what is an Indian baby?
A squawker!

What does a puppy say when it sits on sandpaper?
Ruff!

If a man crosses the ocean twice without taking a bath, what is he called?
A dirty double-crosser!

FARM BOY: My father can't decide whether to get a cow or a tractor.

CITY BOY: He'd look silly riding a cow around.

FARM BOY: He'd look sillier milking a tractor.

LINDA: I've added these figures ten times, Teacher.

TEACHER: Good work, Linda.

LINDA: And here are my ten answers.

A teacher called for sentences using the word "beans."

"My father grows beans," said the bright boy of the class.

"My mother cooks beans," said another pupil.

Then a third popped up: "We are all human beans!"

TEACHER: Say, you can't sleep in my class!

STUDENT: I could if you didn't talk so loud!

"This is really a deep book," said Gertie Giggle. "It's called '20,000 Leagues Under the Sea'."

Two detectives were standing over a dead man named Juan.

1ST DETECTIVE: He was killed with a golf gun.

2ND DETECTIVE: What's a golf gun?

1ST DETECTIVE: I don't know, but it sure made a hole in Juan.

NIT: Is it true that tigers won't hurt you if you run away from them?

WIT: It depends on how fast you run!

PATIENT: What shall I do? I have water on the knee.

TIRED DOCTOR: Wear pumps.

WIFE: Harry! I hear a mouse squeaking!

HUSBAND: Well, what am I supposed to do, get up and oil it?

SQUEEK   SQUEEK

Two leopards in the zoo had just finished their lunch, and one sat back and sighed with contentment, "Mm-mm-mm! that just hit the right spots!"

SAM: Excuse me, but I think you are sitting in my seat.
BIG BRUISER: Oh, yeah, can you prove it?
SAM: I think so. I left my pie and ice cream on it.

FATHER: How do you stand in school?
JIMMY: Right in the corner, as usual!

A gorilla walked into a drugstore and ordered a 50¢ sundae. He put down a ten dollar bill to pay for it. The clerk thought, "Gorillas don't know much about money," and he handed the animal a one dollar bill in change.

The clerk's curiosity got the best of him and he said, "We don't get too many gorillas in here."

The gorilla replied, "No wonder, at nine dollars a sundae!"

MARTIAN BOY: Mom, make me a sandwich, please.

MARTIAN MOTHER (ANGRILY): My goodness, I only have four hands!

NIT: Who was Snow White's brother?

WIT: I don't know.

NIT: Egg white. Get the yolk?

BILL: I had a dream last night that I ate a five-pound marshmallow.

JOE: So what?

BILL: When I woke up, my pillow was gone!

NIT: I've been skating since I was two years old.

WIT: WOW, you must be tired!

If you throw a white hat into the Red Sea, what does it become?

Wet!

If you spot a Navajo seeking a ride on the highway, what season is it?

Indian thumber.

Why do dragons sleep in the daytime?
Because they like to hunt knights.

What did the big rose say to the little rose?
Hiya, bud!

What four letters of the alphabet would frighten a thief?
O I C U.

What animal has two humps and is found in Alaska?
A lost camel.

What three keys won't open doors?
Monkeys, donkeys and turkeys.

What's yellow and wears a mask?
The Lone Lemon.

What is yellow, black, and hot?
Shark-infested mustard!

Why did the little boy put suntan lotion on the chicken?
Because he liked dark meat.

Why did Humpty Dumpty have a great fall?

To make up for a miserable summer.

What has four legs and weighs 1,000 pounds?

Two 500-pound canaries!

TEACHER: Ray, why is your composition on milk only a half-page long when I asked for two pages?

RAY: I wrote on condensed milk.

MAC: Why is your dog staring at me like that?

BETTY: Maybe it's because you're eating out of his dish.

TEXAS BOY: Daddy, I think I'd like to take up the study of stars.

TEXAS FATHER: Good idea! I'll buy Hollywood for you.

TEACHER: Yes, Ann, what is it?

ANN: I don't want to scare you, but Daddy said if I didn't bring home better grades someone is due for a licking!

DORA: In the summer I get up as soon as the first ray of sun comes in at my window.

FLORA: Isn't that rather early?

DORA: No, my window faces west!

NIT: What is the definition of "illegal"?

WIT: A sick bird.

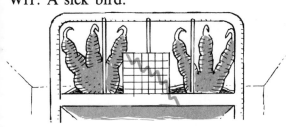

COWBOY: My name is Tex.

DUDE: You must be from Texas.

COWBOY: Nope. I'm from Louisiana, but I couldn't stand the boys calling me Louise!

PETE: My father has Washington's shoe.

TED: That's nothing. My father has Adam's apple.

The human brain is a wonderful thing. It starts working the moment you get up in the morning, and never stops until you're called on in class.

Why can't an elephant ride a bicycle? He has no little finger to ring the bell!

How do you keep an elephant from going through the eye of a needle? Tie a knot in its tail.

Who started the elephant jokes? That's what the elephants want to know!

What goes "Clomp, clomp, clomp, swish—clomp, clomp, clomp, swish"? An elephant with one wet tennis shoe.

Which elephants don't get toothaches? Those in the half of the herd that use Crest.

How do you stop an elephant from charging?
Take away his credit card!

How do you know when an elephant is in your bed?
He has an "E" on his pajamas.

What's the difference between an elephant and peanut butter?
An elephant doesn't stick to the roof of your mouth.

What has two tails, six feet and four trunks?
An elephant with spare parts!

Why do elephants wear sunglasses?
If all those jokes were being told about
  you, you wouldn't want to be rec-
  ognized either.

Isn't it funny that night falls, but day
  breaks?

DAD: If you're good I'll give you a shiny, new penny.

LAD: Haven't you got a dirty, old nickel?

DEENA: Will Miss Issippi wear her New Jersey to the ball?

DINAH: Idaho. Alaska.

MAN: Please give me a ticket to the moon, sir.

AGENT: The moon is full now.

CAL: I was born in South America.

SAL: What part?

CAL: All of me, of course!

"This match won't light."

"What's the matter with it?"

"I don't know. It worked a minute ago."

NIT: Are you going to take the car out in this weather?

WIT: Yes, of course. It's a driving rain, isn't it?

FIRST RACE HORSE: Don't you remember me?

SECOND RACE HORSE: The pace is familiar, but I don't remember the mane.

BILLY: Did you know the bakery is making bread out of yeast and shoe polish?

DAN: No, why?

BILLY: For people who want to rise and shine!

LITTLE GIRL: What is that you're putting on your face?

MOTHER: It's cold cream to make me beautiful.

LITTLE GIRL: It doesn't work, does it?

A man fell from a ten-story building without getting hurt. How come?
He was wearing a light fall suit.

What gives milk and has one horn?
A milk truck!

What did the flower say to the bee?
Quit bugging me!

What's the difference between a hill and a pill?
One's hard to get up, the other's hard to get down!

What animal drops from the clouds?
The rain, dear.

What begins with E and ends with E and has a letter in between?
An envelope.

77

What is the difference between a running man and a running dog?

The man wears trousers and the dog pants.

Why do birds fly south?

Because it's too far to walk.

What is red, white and blue with red dots?

Uncle Sam with the measles.

What keeps a magazine alive?

Good circulation.

What's big, purple and lies across the sea from us?

Grape Britain.

Are you tan from the sun?

No, I'm John Smith from the earth.

RANCHER: What kind of saddle do you want? One with a horn or one without?

DUDE: Without, I guess; you don't have much traffic around here.

NIT: Why do you hope the rain keeps up?

WIT: So it won't come down.

"Did you hear the rope joke?"

"No."

"Skip it."

MOTHER: Where have you been, Johnny? The F.B.I. has been looking for you.

JOHNNY: The F.B.I.?

MOTHER: Yes, *F*ather, *B*rother, and *I*.

Betty was not sitting properly at her school desk. Her feet were out in the aisle, and, besides, she was chewing gum. Said Betty's teacher, "Betty! Take that gum out of your mouth and put your feet in!"

NIT: What book are you reading?
WIT: Speed Reading.
NIT: How long have you been reading it?
WIT: Two years!

JOHN: On the way to school this morning I met a fisherman who hadn't had a bite in a week.
HARRY: What did you do?
JOHN: I bit him.

MOTHER: The best time to take a bath is just before retiring.
JOHNNY: No wonder Grandpa didn't retire until he was sixty-five!